THE
2,000 YEAR OLD MAN
IN THE YEAR 2000

THE 2,000 YEAR OLD MAN IN THE YEAR 2000

IN THE YEAR 2000

 The Book*

INCLUDING HOW TO NOT DIE AND OTHER GOOD TIPS

Mel Brooks *and* Carl Reiner

as told to each other

*Ed. *note*: For greater enjoyment read this book with a Jewish accent. A sample of the authentic accent can be heard on the 2,000 Year Old Man compact discs released by Rhino Records.

Cliff Street Books
An Imprint of HarperPerennial
A Division of HarperCollins*Publishers*

First HarperPerennial edition published 1998.

Designed by Elliott Beard

The Library of Congress has catalogued the hardcover edition as follows:

Brooks, Mel.
    The 2,000 year old man in the year 2000 / by Mel Brooks and Carl Reiner as told to each other. — 1st ed.
        p.   cm.
    ISBN 0-06-017480-3
    1. American wit and humor.   I. Reiner, Carl, 1922–   .
II. Title
PN6162.B73   1997
792.7'028'092—dc21   97-24142

ISBN 0-06-092992-8 (pbk.)

98 99 00 01 02 ❖/RRD 10 9 8 7 6 5 4 3 2 1

To Copernicus,
who worked very closely with me for many years
until we had a falling out about he knows who

Don't go into any water where your feet can't touch the bottom.

—*Pharaoh Totenteetentuttenkamen II*

CONTENTS

PART I
HISTORY & PEOPLE

PART II
HEALTH & FOOD

PART III
MODERN LIFE:
TODAY & TOMORROW

BOOK BONUS
CONTENTS OF THE TABLE

ACKNOWLEDGMENTS

To DAN STRONE, George Shapiro, and Diane Reverand, without whose constant nudging* this book would not have been written.

And thanks to all the people who came to our recording session on February 21 and March 21, 1997, and who with their laughter encouraged us to make another record.

---

*Ed. *note*: Extreme bothering.

AUTHOR'S NOTE

IN 1960 I MET a remarkable man. Following six days of tests at the Mayo Clinic, he came to Los Angeles for a battery of similar exams at UCLA and Cedars Sinai Medical Center. Authorities from these esteemed institutions confirmed what this man claimed in my presence. He was 2,000 years old, the oldest human in the history of man. Nobody had ever lived so long.

Obviously his firsthand knowledge of the past is of immense value to historians, but I think his vast fund of information and unlimited opinions are of equal, if not more, value to ordinary people like you and me who are looking for guidance and reassurance as we face the millennium for the first time.

After all, he's experienced two millenniums, having started life before Christ and lived to witness the Hale-Bopp comet, which his grandparents knew simply as "What the hell was that?"

I had the pleasure of meeting him earlier this year when he came to town for his bicentennial physical, though in truth it's been twenty-four years since I've seen him. At his age, he doesn't move as quickly as he did a few centuries ago.

But even after a long Greyhound bus ride, he was in a great mood. He explained it was because, "the bus has a toilet on it. We don't have to stop in Cincinnati anymore. Any time you feel a woof, you go right in there."

This is his first what he calls "regular-sized" book. Big or little, it doesn't matter. In my opinion, everything in it—every word, anecdote, claim and fact—resonates with truth and importance. You might recognize some of his recollections from our previous conversations. The majority is brand-new. I'm confident it will all be discussed, studied, debated, entered into the Library of Congress, and probably discounted at Wal-Mart.

I hope you enjoy it as much as I do.

Carl Reiner
LOS ANGELES, 1997

INTRODUCTION

HY DID IT TAKE me so long to write my first book?

Well . . .

I'm not using a ghost writer. Or for that matter a *living* writer. I did it myself.

I just sat down with a bottle of ink, a pen, and a ream of unlined paper and I must say it turned out pretty good except for the writing—which was a little slanty.

You need those lines.

At my age, everything's downhill.

I could've published this book sooner, but I had to wait

until I had the proper balance of wit and wisdom. A book with all wit and no wisdom—you're laughing about nothing. A book with all wisdom and no wit . . . you might as well go to the library and take out a book by Schopenhauer.

Or rub sand in your eyes.

Fifty-fifty is what I waited for . . . and a good seven-day diet to put in the book.

Thankfully the method of writing has improved from the days when we used to write on papaya. No, not papyrus. I mean papaya—the fruit. We wrote on them. Not the mushy ones. We used the hard ones. We scratched in the news with a pointy stick. Our motto was, "All the news that's fit to eat."

It was not only informative, it was nutritious. We read it and then we ate it.

Before papaya, we tried writing on onion skin.

It's a shame that wasn't sturdy enough because we had a good motto: "Read it and weep!"

It's the power of the written word.

I like the idea of a book rather than a CD or a cassette.

Did God tell Moses to put the Ten Commandments on a CD or a tape?

No, sir.

He told him to write it down, and that's what I've done here. I've written it down.

Important things should be written down—in stone, if you have the time and the strength.

While I may not be writing with a hammer and chisel, I

hope to capture the whole panorama of my life—from the Table of Contents to the Contents of the Table. I want to tell all. I want to put down the truth, the truth as I knew it. Everything—except maybe some of my private sexual moments with my sixteenth wife, Vilda Chaya.

TTTYOM*

KIEV, 1997

---

*The 2,000 Year Old Man

THE
2,000 YEAR
OLD MAN
IN THE YEAR 2000

PART I

History & People

CHAPTER I

Welcome to Cave 76

HERE IS A LOT to remember. In my time, I've experienced so many diseases, illnesses, and accidents that when I go into the doctor's office for a checkup and get that piece of paper that lists every disease known to medical science, I take a big black crayon and write "Yes" across it. I check them all.

But a medical history, I've learned, is of little value unless it's also accompanied by a personal history. At my most recent checkup, I got X-rays, fluoroscopes, MRIs, CAT scans . . . You name it. Those doctors knew everything about me. Except they couldn't explain my healthy old age.

After every examination, they always asked, "What's the secret to your longevity?"

I was reluctant to divulge. It would only help them and hurt me.

If everyone lived till 2,000, I'd never be able to get a room at the Ramada Inn. They'd all be taken.

But I decided not to be so selfish.

So on with my story . . .

I am a less-than-tall Jewish man with an Eastern European accent and strikingly good-looking for a funny-looking guy. In public I usually wear a black cape and a black hat, and I lean on a cane for balance. In life, balance is good. I'm told that I bear an uncanny resemblance to Mel Brooks. In shopping malls, I get the strangest looks from people who think they recognize me from his movies.

I never saw his movies, but I hear they're very good—I'll have to rent one.

But I'm me, and he's he.

My full name is Benjamin, Ben Aaron, Ben Esau, Ben Solomon, Ben Alvin, Ben Sidney, Ben Lillian (the cross-dresser)—sometimes known as Ben Gay.

Or just say that I've been around. I was born in minus 37 and I lived in a cave with my parents.

It was Cave 76, a roomy cave with southern exposure and an unobstructed view of Cave 75.

Back then a cave was important. It went beyond shelter. It was part of your identity. Every cave was like its own individual nation. We had our own flags and our own national anthems. I'll never forget ours. My mother wrote it. It had such passion and pride. Let me sing it to you. Wait, I'll clear my throat. Here goes:

"Let 'em all go to hell, except Cave 76."

Ha? Is that beautiful?

I still get a chill when I hear that song.

The inside of a cave could be dark, dank, and moist. But ours had two beacons of light and warmth—my parents.

My mother. What can I say about such a wonderful, loving, and caring woman?

She kept busy all day cleaning, cooking, and killing . . . mainly chickens. On Friday nights anything with feathers was a goner. That woman plucked till dawn.

I don't know much about my father. He ate his soup and mumbled his prayers. Basically a quiet Jewish man. But strict. I can still hear him bark, "Candles out at seven!"

I can remember him raising his hand to us kids. But we were never frightened when he raised his hand. It was when he brought it down—that's when we got scared. That's when we ducked and moved.

Everyone said he was a disciplinarian. But believe me, there was no arian* in that man.

My mother and father were typical Jewish parents. Proud

---

*Ed. note: Spelling of "aryan" changed for the joke.

and spiteful. When I was older and could afford my own cave, I invited them over for dinner. It was raining terribly that evening, but my parents wouldn't come in. They stood outside the cave getting wet.

"Come in, Pa," I said.

"No, I'm all right here," he said quietly. "I'm fine."

They were getting drenched by the rain so I yelled at them, "Come in! Come in!"

"We don't have to come in," my mother said. "We can see you from here. We just want to look on you."

Finally I pushed them in and took their coatskins. Then I sat them down and brought dinner.

"No, we already had dinner," my mother said. "We ate some squirrels and berries on the way over. We didn't want to be a bother. We don't ever want you to do anything for us. Just think of yourself, darling. We are nothing."

I realize now they were only doing what all good parents try to do for their children—fill them with guilt for the rest of their lives.

CHAPTER II

My Son, the Doctor

Y CHILDHOOD LASTED 341 years. I was what they call a slow developer, which I believe may have something to do with my longevity. I once heard a leading geriatric specialist propose that a person's long life may be attributed to the slowness of his development. He pointed to turtles and elephants, both of which are slow but have long lives.

I was the slowest of all. I breast-fed for 200 years.

Even after my mother passed on, I continued to nurse. Luckily I was cute and able to con a lot of ladies into feeding me. Bless them, they took pity on me. It was such a thrill. I look back on those as the happiest years of my life. Those were the best meals I ever had.

In those primitive times there was not much work. As a kid, I was lucky to have one of the few jobs available. From morning to night, I took a piece of wood, rubbed it, cleaned it, and then hit a tree with it. Why, you ask? Just to keep busy. There was nothing else to do. But I felt lucky to have that position. There were plenty of people out of work who would've killed for that job.

Later I went to medical school. I'm proud to say that I was the first Jew to study medicine at the big medical cave. It was full of sick and dying people, and it operated on the same principles as modern hospitals. Patients screaming for a doctor, and doctors walking past them with the same indifference as today. We invented that procedure.

In those days medical school wasn't so difficult. There wasn't too much to learn. Mainly we learned how to be diagnosticians. They taught us to stick our finger up a patient's nose. If he didn't holler, "Hey, get your finger outta my nose," then we knew he was dead and threw him out of the cave to make room for new patients.

I graduated in a week. My parents were so proud. My mother was the first one in history to say, "This is my son, the doctor." She coined that phrase.

I found a cave and hung up my shingle outside. I lived and worked there until I was suddenly dispossessed—not by a landlord . . . by a lion.

A landlord I could deal with. But with a lion, there is no

hondling.* We made a deal. He walked in, and I got out. I didn't even argue.

"It's your cave," I said. "Just step away from the opening, Leo, and let me out. And I'd appreciate it if you didn't try to eat me when I go by."

After that I lived in many places. I lived in hovels, in wigwams, in mud huts, in straw huts, in stone huts . . . I lived in all kinds huts.

But I must say the happiest days of my life were spent at 1142 Sutton Place South, New York, New York 10021. What a building. You never saw such a lobby. It had a beautiful fountain with running water and colored lights. First the water was red, then the water was blue, then red again, then blue again, then red again, then blue again . . . amazing! To this day I don't know how they did that.

I lived in the building for a year and a half until once again I was dispossessed. But not by the lions. This time by the wolves.

Izzy and Irene Wolfe.

I was subletting, and they came back from their European vacation a month early.

---

*Ed. *note:* Bargaining.

CHAPTER III

The All Mighty

VEN BEFORE THE All Mighty, I believed in a superior being. His name was Phil.

Out of respect we called him Philip. Philip was big and strong like an ox. He had a big red beard, a chest like a barrel, and arms the size of two oak trees. Nobody was as powerful as Philip. If he wanted, he could kill you. As a result, we revered him and we prayed to him.

"Oooh, Philip, please don't hurt us. Don't pinch us. Please don't take our eyes out."

But one day Phil was hit by a bolt of lightning.

All of a sudden we looked up in the sky and said, "There's something bigger than Phil!"

From then on, we paid allegiance to the new Lord who

was more powerful than Phil. We called him "Oy gevalt!" which in ancient Hebrew means, "WOW!"

The news got around fast. It was delivered by the town Crier, who ran by the caves and hovels yelling the news.

"Philip was killed by a crooked light from the sky! Oy, gevalt!"

"Oy, Mookie was eaten by a lion!"

"Oy-oy-oy! Heshie's wife ran away with a Roman gladiator. Oy vey!"

All that crying—it took so much out of the Crier. To help out, we hired a morning Crier, a six o'clock Crier, and an eleven o'clock Crier.

I was a town Crier in Sodom for a while. Or was it Gomorra? Doesn't matter. It didn't last too long. A lot of people complained that they couldn't understand the news because of my Jewish accent. But I got rid of that a couple of centuries later. I explain how in another chapter. Read on.

CHAPTER IV

Fire

 REMEMBER WHAT big news it was when Murray discovered fire. He was standing under a tree one afternoon when that crooked light from the sky, the same one that killed Phil, hit a tree and caught it on fire. It also set Murray on fire. He ran into the cave screaming, "Fire! Fire!"

I leaped to my feet and shouted, "Everyone get your marshmallows on your sticks! Hurry! Hurry!"

Then we all rushed at Murray. We shoved so many marshmallows all at once, we put him out. Of course, Murray was delighted not to be on fire anymore.

But we were stuck with cold marshmallows. Those were hard days for everyone.

CHAPTER V

Infomercials

ES, WE HAD infomercials back then. My cousin Moishe—little Mershel—invented them 1,100 years ago.

Mershel, a smart boy who was loaded with information, came into your hovel late at night when you were sound asleep. He started to talk fast and furious. He woke you up and before you knew where you were or who you were, he began to sell.

"Folks, I got what you need, something that will make your life worth living . . . it's called a digital extender!"

Hmm, a digital extender, we thought. It sounded interesting.

Then Mershel showed us the digital extender.

It was a plain stick! From a tree! The kind anybody could get.

But that was Mershel's genius, his brilliance as a salesman. He sold it.

"With this digital extender, you can get someone's attention," he explained. "You can use it to write love letters in the sand. If you get an itch in the back, the digital extender will remove it. Or if a big stranger comes into your hovel, you can poke him in the gentles."*

That sold me.

I bought two—one for the week and one with a snakeskin handle for the weekend.

Because of Mershel, we invented the remote control—a rock.

When Mershel became too annoying, we threw it at him. We heard a click, and he went out.

---

*Ed. *note:* genitals.

Author's *note:* No, *gentles,* from gently—how a man's private parts should be treated.

CHAPTER VI

The Height Report

ONE OF US KNEW from modern measurements. We didn't have feet, inches, meters, or centimeters. We took the measurements with our hands.

For men, it was simple. Most were eleven or twelve hands tall.

With women, it was more complicated. We never found out how tall they were. We'd start measuring the ladies down at their toes. By the time we got up to their thighs, the measuring turned into fondling. We tried measuring from the head down, but that was even worse. As soon as the hand reached the nipple, we got horizontal—and that was the end of the measuring.

To this day I couldn't tell you the height of any of the women from that era.

CHAPTER VII

Close to 500 Wives

 OU'VE HEARD OF marriages of convenience? In my time, they were all like that.

We asked ourselves, "What do you need a woman for?"

It was for convenience and necessity. Unless you had eyes in the back of your head, which would've been a rare occurrence, you needed a woman to keep a lookout if an animal was creeping up behind you. So we said, "Lady, will you look behind me for a while?"

"How long?" she'd ask.

"Forever."

"OK."

And that was it. A simple ceremony.

We were married.

I've been married close to 500 times. Of those marriages, 71 percent were absolutely perfect. The other 29 percent? Squabbles, squabbles, and squabbles.

"Don't eat your soup with your fork."

"Don't leave your sandals by the cave entrance."

"Why can't we live in a hovel as nice as the Joneses'?"

"Must you always leave your dirty animal skins on the bathroom floor?"

It was always something.

But I have wonderful memories of many of my wives. My first wife, Anna, gave up her virginity to give me my manhood. As for the others, well . . . Naomi, she should rest in peace, never nagged me to take out the goat. Ruth, God bless her, never had a headache. Miriam, such a gentle soul, never served me a cold meal. Esther, she should rest in peace, never spoke with her mouth full.

And then there was Muriel, who taught me the meaning of unbridled hatred, and Jezebel, who made me appreciate Muriel. Bessie, an unhappy woman—day and night she sang the blues. Back then they were called *tsurus* songs. All day long she sang:

> *Baby, baby, baby*
> *That's all you want from me*
> *If you make me make mo' babies*
> *I'm leaving on the 5:03 . . .*

She never left. She just kept singing.

I may have set some sort of record for longevity with my marriage to Rebecca. We were together eighty-one years— from 1000 to 1081. No trouble. She never uttered a cross word. Never uttered any word—till her deathbed when she said, "I'm going now."

My briefest marriage lasted one day. It was to Bernice Zolotov, and I still get upset thinking about that one. Three main things went wrong with this alliance. First I found out that she was a rotten cook and she was too religious. Everything she made was either a sacrifice or a burnt offering.* Then she tells me that she doesn't do windows . . . or floors or ceilings.

I could've overlooked all of that.

The day we were married I knew something was wrong. I could feel it in my heart. But on our wedding night I felt it not only in my heart but in my hand. Bernice turned out to be Bernie. What a shock!

He was the most gorgeous of all my wives. Big blue eyes, long lashes . . .

That fateful evening started so beautifully. We had tender and beautiful kissing . . . such kissing I'd never experienced. Tiny gentle touches on the lips. With my eyes closed, I could imagine a little bird kissing me. It never stopped.

Kiss-kiss-kiss-kiss-kiss . . .

Such erotic kissing.

---

*Ed. note: Henny Youngman, Grossinger's Hotel, 1940, used without his permission.

A little tongue, a little kiss, a little tongue, a little kiss . . .

The best kissing of my life.

Bernie loved me from the deepest part of him. There was no question about that. It was heartbreaking when I told him that he had to leave. He stood outside the house screaming, "I'll learn to cook. I'll do the floors."

A moment later, he added, "I'll get circumcised!"

Another shock—Bernie was a gentile!

For a moment I considered the offer. Bernie was tall, and it's hard to find someone who's so tall and attractive. Maybe, I thought, when they circumcised him, if they took away a lot. Maybe the whole thing . . .

But no, no, I let him go.

From then on I had an acceptance for homosexuals. Almost a kinship. I was a maverick in that respect. To this day, the gay community and I understand each other. We have more than just our love for Judy Garland in common. We also love Bette Midler.

I wish my sixty-sixth wife, Zenobia, had had such affection for me. We lived in a town where streets were canals filled with water. The country didn't even have a name. It was so beautiful. I remember strolling on the Rialto in San Marco Square and saying to Zenobia, "The people here, they look so Italian. I've never seen such Italian-looking people. They should call this place Italy."

I told everyone my suggestion. But they didn't listen. They called it Venice.

Years later I was vindicated. They called the whole country Italy. I feel good about that.

I thought Zenobia and I had such a good marriage. Then one beautiful summer day she took off. She ran away right after we had lunch with this fella, Lord Byron. He was so handsome and romantic. Everything he said was, "Hark . . . Hark, look yonder . . . Hark, the birds. Hark the trees. Hark the sky."

He harked her right out of my life.

But I've been lucky in love, too. I've known some wonderful women. You've probably heard of Helen of Troy? Don't get ahead of yourself. I didn't marry Helen. I married her sister, Janice. Janice Troy.

But it's in the family, right?

I mean, Helen was around the house all the time.

I saw her practically every day . . . sometimes in her skivvies.*

I was always saying, "Hi, Helen."

"How're you doing, Helen?"

"Launch any ships today, Helen?"

It's true what they said about her looks. Helen's face launched over a thousand ships.

Janice wasn't as pretty. But she had a body that launched a few canoes.

She was also a sensational kisser.

As good as Bernie, you ask?

If you had kissed Bernie, you wouldn't have to ask.

---

*Ed. *note*: Bloomers.

CHAPTER VIII

Salome &
Premature Ejaculation

 DATED SALOME—YES, the remarkable beauty from the Bible. We might've married, but I found out that I couldn't have children with her. It wasn't that I was impotent. *Au contraire.* I was opulent. I had a full tank.

It's just that Salome did that famous dance of hers with the seven veils. Such a wonderful, sensual dance you've never seen. With each veil, that little firecracker revealed more of herself. By the fourth veil, her belly button showed. It was so adorable, it drove me crazy.

I couldn't last the seven veils.

By the time she got to the fifth veil, I became premature.

So there was no way to have children. Unfortunately, back then they didn't collect the sperm in test tubes and store it till later like they do today. In those days they just cleaned it up. When I talk like this people ask if it's wishful thinking or if I can still produce semen.

All I can tell you is I've got two boys in the Navy. Able-bodied semen.* Both first-class.

---

*Ed. *note:* Seamen.

CHAPTER IX

42,000 Kids

I HAVE MORE than 42,000 children.

And not one comes to visit me.

But they're children. All you can do is let them go.

I say, "Good luck to them."

Let them be happy. As long as they're happy, I don't care.

Of course, they could send a note.

"Hiya, Pop. Howya doing, Pop?"

I'm proud of them anyway. I have 21,000 doctors, 10,000 lawyers, 700 accountants, 400 teachers, plenty of scientists, a few rabbis, and the rest are in show business (ten Oscars, twenty-two Golden Globes, seven Emmys, sixteen Tonys, two Obies, and a Kasha.*)

All the great Jewish entertainers gave their parents their awards to put on top of their TV sets. My set is full up. It all started with Moses, who gave his mother and father the stone tablets with the Ten Commandments on them. They went right over the mantelpiece with a beautiful forty-dollar gold-leaf frame around them.

You couldn't walk into that home without his mother saying, "Look what my Moses brought us from his trip to the mountains."

*Author's note: Russian award for country-eastern singing.

CHAPTER X

A Very Good Book

'M A RELIGIOUS MAN. It may be one of the reasons for my longevity. Every morning, I get out of bed and open the window. I stand in my shorts—my 100 percent cotton Fruit of the Loom boxers (boxers are better than briefs; they allow your gentles* to breathe)—and I inhale and then I exhale. Inhale and exhale twelve times.

---

*Ed. *note*: Genitals.

Author's note: If you read my note on gentles, you'll know that gentles are always gentles. Don't you read my notes? I read yours.

Then I fall to my knees and pray fiercely for twenty-two minutes that the ceiling shouldn't fall on me or my heart should not attack me.

I also pray that I shouldn't be attacked for what I'm going to reveal next: The Bible, a *very* good book, an all-time best-seller, is full of exaggerations. I knew the Bible's head writer, Shem. He lived two caves away from me. A lovely, talented man, he worked with a small staff. They took stories from the news and pepped them up.

What Shem did with Noah's Ark is a masterpiece. According to what he wrote, it rained for forty days and forty nights.

Don't believe it.

It rained four days and four nights. It was a bad storm, not the end of the world.

But Shem knew how to grab people's attention, and keep it. Let me ask you this: You're standing in front of two movie theaters. One is showing a movie called *The Typhoon*, and the other has *It's Drizzling*. Which are you going to pay to see?

Shem also built up the story about Moses parting the Red Sea. From what I recall, Moses didn't part a thing. He didn't even part his hair. Look at his pictures. When Pharaoh was chasing the Jews, Moses led his people to a secret shallow spot in the Red Sea that he knew about and said, "Hurry, hurry! Cross here! Cross here!"

Shem knew that he'd lose readers if he reported how easy it was. He wanted to sell Bibles. So he rewrote it as a very dramatic chase, and you've got to hand it to him. As adventure stories go, Exodus is a classic. You can't beat it.

But I don't mean to denigrate Moses. He was always a

heckuva hero. People wrote about him long before Shem ever did. When I was a little boy the first book I ever read was about Moses. I'll never forget that book. I slept with it every night. It was called *Zechum Mochum Roochum*—in ancient Hebrew that means *See Moses Run*.

It was a real page-turner. In fact, I still have that little book. I've kept it all these centuries. Look:

SEE MOSES!

SEE PHARAOH!

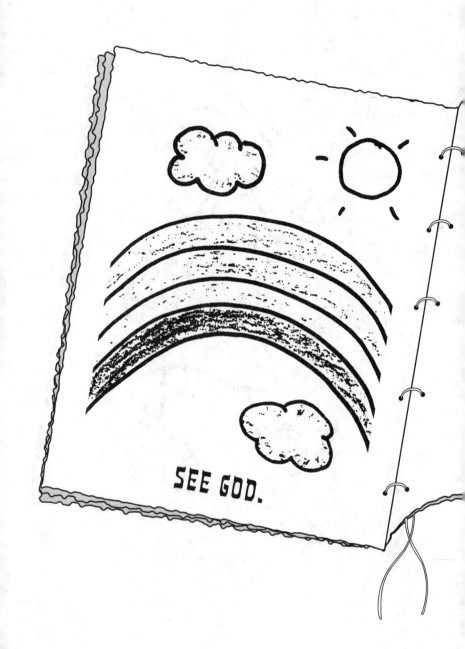

SEE GOD THROW A STICK.

SEE THE STICK
TURN INTO A SNAKE!

CHAPTER XI

Moses Comes Clean

 HERE WAS SOMETHING about Moses that Shem never wrote about. Many years after bringing the Ten Commandments down from Mount Sinai, Moses made a startling confession. Originally he'd been given three tablets, containing a total of fifteen commandments. While struggling with that heavy load, he dropped one, destroying five of the commandments.

Moses kept quiet. I don't think he feared God as much as he hated *schlepping* up that mountain again.

Not me. I was curious. I hiked up that mountain and found those broken pieces. I put it back together like a jigsaw puzzle.

Finally, I got one commandment done. It was a special moment. For the first time since God presented the commandments to Moses, another human being would read them. After taking a deep breath, I stood back and beheld the words:

I was so disappointed. I looked down at the broken pieces of the other commandments and realized Moses probably dropped the third tablet not because it was heavy, but because they didn't have the majesty or the wisdom of the first ten.

Besides being a great leader, Moses was the world's first editor.

CHAPTER XII

Merchandising

S SOON AS religion caught on, I opened my first factory. I manufactured Mogen Davids, Stars of David. I was the first to mass produce them. I figured the six-pointed star would be a popular item, and I guessed right.

Everybody wanted one. I employed six men. Each one held a large, heavy point in his arms and ran at top speed into the middle of the room. The intense heat generated from crashing together fused the pieces into a Jewish star.

The most we made was two stars a day—because of the many accidents. After all, six men running at each other with points, you're going to have a few mishaps. Between the medical bills and the new religions that were springing up in those days, I was lucky to break even.

A couple of years later, I missed out on an offer to be a partner in a new business. Simon, a local fella, came to see me with a brand-new product.

"We have a new thing, a new item," he explained. "It looks like a winner, like something that could be a big seller."

He showed me a simple wooden thing. Two sticks.

"It's called a cross," he added.

I looked at it carefully. Turned it over. Inspected all sides.

"It's simple," I said. "*Too* simple . . . I'm afraid it's not stylish."

Go know! That design became a classic that's been copied and reproduced in countless ways for centuries. You see it everywhere. It's on top of churches, cemeteries, and in every Dracula movie. I thought it was too simple. I didn't know it was eloquent. If I had started making crosses, I could've dropped four employees . . . just two guys run together and BANG, you've got a cross.

I wish I would've been smarter . . . but I'm no dummy either. You don't see me putting on a pair of black Nike sneakers and booking a seat on a spaceship behind a comet.

CHAPTER XIII

I Knew Jesus

 KNEW JESUS before they named a religion after him. I had a little candy store just outside of Bethlehem and he came in all the time but he never bought anything. He always asked me for a glass of water. Who knew this thin, thirsty lad would shake up the world one day? Not me. If I'd known that, I'd have made him a partner in the store!

The Jesus I knew was nothing like the way he's depicted in *Jesus Christ Superstar*—both the play and the movie. They've made a travesty of his behavior. Jesus would never have knocked over tables, punched moneylenders, or screamed at anyone. He didn't sing either. He was quiet. He wore sandals.

A nice boy. He talked softly but never carried a big stick. Just a big heart. He liked working with his hands.

Everyone knows he was a carpenter, but what people don't know is how good a carpenter he was.

I can tell you this firsthand: He was the best.

Jesus once made a knotty pine cabinet for me. It had three drawers, and two little ones at the top. Real craftsmanship. He charged me 150 cisterstes*—worth about two and a half cents in today's money.

I asked if I could give him a check, and he said, "Sure, just make it out to Jesus. I have faith in you."

He had faith in everybody. What a guy!

---

*Author's note: In Spartacus, Laurence Olivier bought Kirk Douglas from Peter Ustinov for 1,000 cisterstes.

CHAPTER XIV

Yarmulkes Galore

LITTLE MORE than 1,000 years later, I moved to Madrid and opened a store, a darling little hat shop called Yarmulkes Galore. I carried beautiful yarmulkes—all sizes and all types. Every Jewish guy had one. These skullcaps flew out of the store like Frisbees, and you may be surprised to hear that it had nothing to do with religion. The whole yarmulke craze was due to a young rabbi's vanity.

Then as now, in orthodox Jewish temples, the women sat up in the balcony and looked down upon the rabbi. Our young rabbi suffered from premature male pattren* baldness. He was ashamed for the ladies to see his shiny bald spot. So before one Friday night service, he took a piece of black cloth, cut out a small circle, licked it like a stamp, and stuck it on his bald spot.

What happened next was the beginning of a fad. A couple of kids started and before you know it everyone jumps on the bandwagon, just like the kids today who wear their baseball caps backwards. Soon other men in the congregation thought it looked cool. They said, "This is a happening. It must be the thing. I want to be with it, too. Where do you get one?"

The minute I heard, "Where do you get one," I opened Yarmulkes Galore. With a big sign in front:

YOU GET THEM HERE!

The shop was a hit and remained popular until the big crash—which you know as the Spanish Inquisition.

That was some crash. In one day they destroyed 10,000 yarmulkes—not to mention the Jews under them.

It was bad. Bad for them, bad for me. We all suffered.

---

*Ed. note: Pattern.

---

*Author's note: If they'd been reading this with a Jewish accent as you told them to, you wouldn't need this note.

CHAPTER XV

One Crazy Jew

T THAT TIME, I saw many people deny their religion to stay alive. Some of my best customers went with the flow. They made whatever accommodations they had to.

Not me. I wouldn't give in to those Nogoodniks.

The Grand Inquisitor had me arrested and brought in for questioning. They were all there—the Grand Inquisitor, the Petty Inquisitor, all the Inquisitors. They hung me up on a wall in chains, and the Petty Inquisitor, the sarcastic one, asked, "Comfortable?"

"I make a nice living,"* I quipped.

The Grand Inquisitor wasn't amused. He shouted, "Are you a Jew?"

I thought for a long time and said, "Is the air conditioning on?"

I was trying to change the subject but no such luck.

He continued, "Do you deny your faith?"

I paused again.

"What do you mean . . . deny?"

"Will you recant your faith?" the Inquisitor snarled.

"What do you mean . . . recant?"

"Will you *change* your faith?"

"What do you mean . . . your?"

I was thinking it over when a big hairy guy came over to me with a red hot poker.

The Grand Inquisitor said, "Unless you say that you want to be a Christian and don't want to be a Jew anymore, we are going to shove this red-hot poker up your tush."

Well, I must admit that was an incentive, but I didn't recant. Instead I screamed at the top of my lungs.

"Go ahead! Shove it up my tush! Get *another* guy with *another* red-hot poker and shove it down my throat! Meet in the middle and make me a rotisserie Jew! I'm not afraid of you! Go ahead, stick it in my ear! Stick it up my nose! Scramble my brain! I love pain! Give me all you got!"

---

*Ed. note: Myron Cohen, the *Ed Sullivan Show*, 1951, CBS, used without his permission.

There was silence. The Grand Inquisitor pointed a finger at me, turned to the other Inquisitors, and said, "This is some crazy Jew. If we convert him, we'll have a crazy Christian. Better he should be a Jew. *Luzim gayen!*"*

---

*Ed. *note:* "Let him go!" from Mel Brooks as Indian Chief in his movie *Blazing Saddles,* 1974.

Author's note: I rent this video at least once a month—it's hysterical.

CHAPTER XVI

What the Hell Are *You* Looking At?

FTER THAT Spanish Inquisition, which was a traumatic experience, I learned something important—how to handle a bully. I turned a negative into a positive by writing a self-help book which I titled *What the Hell Are* You *Looking* At? The Inquisition is long gone, but there's always going to be a guy in a bar or a subway who'll turn to you, and say, "What the hell are *you* looking at?"

My book gives the technique for dealing with those kinds of guys. Since it's hard to find the book, I'll boil it down for you to the basic philosophy. If someone asks in a loud voice, "What the hell are you looking at?" you reply in a louder voice, "I'm looking at you, shithead." That makes them think you're crazier than they are and they back off.

CHAPTER XVII

Wonders of the World

 NTIL RECENTLY, I was like everyone else—convinced there were just Seven Wonders of the World. I'd visited them all personally myself—the Hanging Gardens of Babylon, the Temple of Artemis at Ephesus, the Colossus of Rhodes, the Pyramids of Egypt, the Tomb of Mausolus at Halicarnassus, the Statue of Zeus at Olympia, the Pharos of Alexandria. All good wonders, wonderful wonders.

But just lately I discovered one in this century that *must* be added to the list.

As far as I'm concerned, it's definitely the Eighth Wonder of the World, and when you see it I know you wouldn't argue. In the first place, the other Wonders of the World you have to travel far and wide to see. *My* Wonder you don't have to travel to. It's on four continents and in thirty-six convenient locations.

What am I talking about?

I'm talking about Planet Hollywood! The Eighth Wonder of the World!

Oh my God, what they're doing there! Nine ninety-five for a hamburger that could feed an army. And what they got there. Classic movies on every wall. The motorcycle from *Easy Rider* hanging there. Costumes from the great stars in their great hits—Vivien Leigh's dress from *Gone with the Wind*, John Wayne's eye patch from *True Grit*, Arnold Schwarzenegger's jock strap from *Terminators I* and *II* (he wore the same one in both pictures).

What don't they have there you wouldn't be interested in.

Not only memorabilia, but celebrities!

When I was at the Hanging Gardens of Babylon did I see Bruce and Demi hanging around there? No sir! They're hanging around Planet Hollywood! Along with other big stars. When I walked inside the other night, I couldn't believe who I saw in a corner booth, talking to his friends. I gasped. I couldn't breathe. I started to get a little dizzy. I almost fainted.

It was Rocky . . . himself!

Sly.

Yes, Sylvester Stallone.

It took a few moments for me to regain my composure. I had to meet this man. You know, I'm getting nervous just writing about it. Anyway, I summoned my courage, went over to him, and stammered like a schoolgirl.

"Hey, hey, Rocky," I said. "How ... how about an autograph?"

And do you know what he said to me?

Rocky looked right at me and said, "Fuck you!"

For a second I was stunned. But I don't blame him. I know how many people must annoy him with such requests. My night was already made. A big hamburger and a big star like Rocky saying to me, "Fuck you." I was in heaven ...

People question me when I tell them this story. They say, "It doesn't sound like our Rocky. Rocky is so sweet and he doesn't talk that way."

I don't know, maybe it wasn't him. Maybe it was an emulator.*

Now that I think about it, it could have been an emulator ...

Let it be an emulator. Who needs a lawsuit? It was definitely an emulator saying "Fuck you."

---

*Ed. *note:* Rather than emulator, wouldn't more people understand the word "impersonator"?

Author's *note:* Probably.

Ed. *note:* Don't you feel you're using the f-word too frequently?

Author's *note:* Fuck you.

CHAPTER XVIII

Conversation with a Hollywood Pest

VERY TIME I TRAVEL to California, this Hollywood pest, Carl Reiner, finds me wherever I am and insists on asking me questions about my life. He loves to ask questions and doesn't stop until I answer. And he's such an obsessive-compulsive when it comes to the truth. Always backing me into a corner.

When he heard I was writing a book, Mr. Reiner suggested sharing portions of our tape-recorded conversations. I thought about it and it seemed like not such a bad idea. And so . . .

CARL REINER: Sir, I glanced through some of the pages you've written and I'm amazed. Although I've known you for many years, this is the first time I've known you to use the f-word.

THE 2,000 YEAR OLD MAN: Well, over the last thirty years or so, I've been liberated. Mainly by Martin Scorsese.

CR: He freed you up?

TTTYOM: Yes, I'm now comfortable with those filthy words.

CR: Because of his movies?

TTTYOM: Yes, sir. At the beginning, I was shocked. You don't expect to hear, "Don't fuck with me. I'll fuck with you." "Did you want to fuck my wife? I don't want to fuck your wife." "You fuck my sister, I'll fuck your sister." It's terrible and shocking, but after a while, it's refreshing.

CR: You feel a freedom—

TTTYOM: Yes, I'm liberated. Now I'm not afraid to go to any of those "Fuck You" parties where people are saying, "Fuck you." When they give me a "Fuck you," I give them a "Fuck you" right back. It's fun. I'm with it, Baby.

CR: That's wonderful.

TTTYOM: Yes, I love it.

CR: You mentioned the Scorsese movies. So you like going to the movies?

TTTYOM: I love the movies. I love sitting in these new movie complexes, these twelve plexes, where I can watch a movie and hear two others on each side of me. You get a lot. You know what's going on in every movie. It's a pleasure. Plus, I pay half-price. I'm a senior, you know.

CR: You're at least a senior.

TTTYOM: Now that you mention it, the price for seniors is not fair. At sixty, half-price is OK, but if somebody's seventy-five they should let them in for a dollar and maybe give them a hat, too—with the name of the movie on it.

CR: What about at one hundred?

TTTYOM: If you're one hundred or over, you should get in for free. With a large drink and a tub of popcorn. Maybe even one of them giant chocolate bars, the kind you can panel your den with.

CR: And what about at your age?

TTTYOM: Me? Me, they should give a thousand dollars for every *Twister* and *Volcano* that I have to sit through. And two thousand dollars for another Batman movie.

CR: I was thinking you have so many wonderful insights and so much knowledge, I'm amazed that you haven't written your autobiography sooner.

TTTYOM: We have Mr. Dickens to thank for that.

CR: Charles Dickens?

TTTYOM: Yes.

CR: You knew him?

TTTYOM: Knew him? Sure. He gave me a Chanukah present once. A pen and ink set. Chuck was my pal.

CR: You called him Chuck?

TTTYOM: I call all my Charleses Chuck: Chuck Darwin, Chuck Chaplin, Chuck de Gaulle, and let's not leave out King Chuck the Second.

CR: You and Charles Dickens exchanged Chanukah presents?

TTTYOM: Not exchanged. He gave me that present out of guilt.

CR: What was he guilty about?

TTTYOM: You want the unvarnished truth?

CR: Of course.

TTTYOM: Charles Dickens stole one of my stories.

CR: Which story?

TTTYOM: A *Tale of Two Shtetls.**

CR: That sounds like A *Tale of Two Cities.*

TTTYOM: He stole it—almost word for word. The original cities were Minsk and Pinsk. He changed it to London and Paris to disguise it. But the story is mine.

CR: What was yours about?

TTTYOM: Mine was about a little Jewish tailor from Minsk who invented the notched lapel, and his brother-in-law from Pinsk who stole the pattren and took the credit.

CR: But A *Tale of Two Cities* is about the French Revolution and the aristocrats who were guillotined.

TTTYOM: So he put a twist on it. I was so disappointed and angry by this that I threw the pen-and-ink set into the Thames. It was more than a century before I could bring myself to write again. It really got my nose out of joint.

CR: Since you mentioned your nose, sir, I've been looking at it for a while, and I'm absolutely amazed. Your face seems to be ageless. I hope I'm not being too personal, but have you ever had plastic surgery?

TTTYOM: You're looking at a pioneer in the field of rhino-plasty.

---

*Ed. *note:* Villages.

CR: Are you telling me that you've had a nose job?

TTTYOM: Who else would I be telling? You're the only one here with me.

CR: Sir, I don't mean to be impolite, but if you did have rhinoplasty they left you with a rather substantial nose. They didn't take off very much, did they?

TTTYOM: Are you kidding? You're looking at a button compared to what I had.

CR: I can't believe it. Your nose was bigger?

TTTYOM: My nose used to enter a room two minutes before I arrived. They always knew I was coming when they saw the tip of that nose.

CR: It must have been an encumbrance.

TTTYOM: It was good and bad. I made a living with that nose.

CR: How?

TTTYOM: Playing Cyrano de Bergerac. I created the role.

CR: Is this true, sir?

TTTYOM: Read the reviews. Look them up! Bosley Bullshit, the criticizer from *Le Figaro*, wrote, "Rostand has written a marvelously entertaining play, marred only by the leading actor's insistence on wearing a ridiculously oversized fake nose and speaking in an anti-Semitic Jewish accent."

CR: You remember the review?

TTTYOM: An actor never forgets terrible reviews.

CR: You must've been hurt by this review?

TTTYOM: I was wounded. It stung me deeply. That rotten criticizer drove me to a plastic surgeon.

CR: That was so cruel of him.

TTTYOM: Cruel? That was the only nice thing he ever did for me.

CR: What was nice about it?

TTTYOM: I told you, he drove me to the plastic surgeon. When he saw that it was my real nose, he immediately apologized and said, "Get in the carriage. We have no time to lose." And he drove me to the plastic surgeon.

CR: Did you ever forgive him for calling your accent anti-Semitic?

TTTYOM: Of course. He also drove me to an elocution teacher. Thanks to him, I ended up talking like everyone else. Some people think I sound like Dan Rather.

CR: You don't sound like Dan Rather to me.

TTTYOM: And some people, like you, say I don't sound like Dan Rather. I'm not going to get in the middle of that one. Everybody's a Henry Higgins.

CR: Sir, having known so many great authors—Dickens and Rostand—you must be an avid reader.

TTTYOM: I've read everything he ever wrote.

CR: Who?

TTTYOM: Ovid.

CR: No, I said "avid."

TTTYOM: Who's Avid?

CR: Avid is not a he. It's a word. It means "enthusiastic."

TTTYOM: All right, put me down for an avid Ovid reader. I love Ovid. He's still one of my favorite writers.

CR: What did you love so much about him?

TTTYOM: He was a great poet. He wrote about the truth of society—the highs, the lows, and the mediums. He loved sex and wrote about it graphically. Too graphically. Which made Emperor Augustus very nervous. The Emperor sent his aide to talk to Ovid. He said to him, "Emperor Augustus wants you to take out a little of the 'Let me shove it in here' and the 'Let me shove it in there.'" Ovid said, "Tell your Emperor that I'm an artist. If I write, 'I'll shove it up there,' it's gonna stay 'up there.'" The Emperor was furious, and had Ovid summarily thrown out of the court. It was in the newspaper.

CR: What newspaper?

TTTYOM: The *Roman Tribune.* I'll never forget that headline: OVID OUSTED, AUGUSTUS DISGUSTED!

CR: That sounds like a headline from *Variety*—from when Disney let Michael Ovitz go.

TTTYOM: Yes, but my Ovid didn't get such a wonderful departure package. My Ovid got kicked in the ass and thrown in the Euphrates.

CR: As long as we're talking about people, you have known some of the most famous in history. For instance, I'd love to hear about your involvement with Joan of Arc.

TTTYOM: I'm sure you would ... Ah, Joan, Joan, Joan. We had such a wonderful relationship. Very different, very strange—how should I say it without besmirching her holy saintliness? I loved her so much. That poor girl.

CR: Where did you meet her?

TTTYOM: At a bar—

CR: At a bar?

TTTYOM: Let me finish. At a bar mitzvah. One of her offi-
cers, a Captain Dreyfus, was a friend of mine, and he invited me to his son Max's bar mitzvah.

CR: Was it love at first sight?

TTTYOM: Maybe for her, but I feel stupid to tell you that I
didn't even know Joan was a girl. She was a general with
armor, riding on a horse, and carrying a big sword. And
my friend, Captain Dreyfus, said in his thick French accent, "*Je veux vous introduire Jeanne D'Arc.*" I thought I was
being introduced to "John Dark." That's how the Captain
pronounced it. And I just thought that John was a very,
very handsome guy . . . just this side of beautiful. That
night we became pals, and he invited me to join his army.

CR: As a what?

TTTYOM: A utility man. I did everything. I was a sword
sharpener, a pharmacist . . . and I cleaned and pressed
their chain mail garments . . . not easy. Anyway, for
months we were together—John fighting and killing and
me sharpening and filling prescriptions. All day I
thought of him and every time I saw him riding on that
white horse I felt stirrings. I began to have disturbing
thoughts about my sexuality even though I'd already been
married a couple hundred times and I did have that up-
setting experience with Bernie Zolotov. I'd heard about
married men suddenly making a left turn. I didn't want to
take that turn. But for my John . . .

CR: What happened?

TTTYOM: One day Johnny came marching home and said to
me, "This is such a long war, and it's so hot on that battle-

field. I need a bath." "We both could use one," I said. So I went with him and we rented a room in a quaint little countryside inn. Johnny couldn't wait to get into a hot tub. He took off his armor and his underwear, and I looked at him with amazement. "Hey, John," I asked, "what happened to you?" You know, I'd always liked Jeanne d'Arc, but from that moment I loved him and I told him/her so, but it didn't work out. Jeanne was married to her career. She was always saying, "I've got to go save France." I didn't feel so patriotic, so I told her, "All right, you save France. I'll wash up." We both served our country—her in her way, me in mine.

CR: That's quite a story. Is there any evidence to authenticate that it's true?

TTTYOM: Every time I talk to you, you have this paranoid thing with the truth. Everything's got to be the truth.

CR: Well, you tell me things about historical figures—it's important to know if it's the truth.

TTTYOM: The truth, the truth, the truth! If I told you the truth, could you handle it?

CR: I could, sir. I could handle it.

TTTYOM: All right, let's see. Remember all those things I told you about Moses?

CR: Yes.

TTTYOM: Well, what if I told you Moses wasn't Jewish?

CR: WHAT?

TTTYOM: He was really an Egyptian.

CR: Wait—wait—wa—wa—

TTTYOM: Wa—wa—wa—wa—wa—wa! See, you're trembling. You're shaking. You're stuttering. YOU CAN'T HANDLE THE TRUTH!

CR: But it's not the truth—

TTTYOM: So what. That's not the point. I just wanted to see if you could handle the truth if it was the truth, and I don't think you can. You got red in the face.

CR: So did you, and I'm sorry I got you excited. At your age, it's not a good idea to get that angry.

TTTYOM: It's OK. Anger is good. It helps the circulation in my arteries, my veins, and my small caterpillars.

CR: That's capillaries.

TTTYOM: Not caterpillars?

CR: No, capillaries.

TTTYOM: You sure?

CR: I'm sure.

TTTYOM: You swear to God?

CR: Yes, the word is "capillaries."

TTTYOM: All right, from now on, I'll say capillaries.

CR: So you think anger is good for circulation?

TTTYOM: I know it is. When I get very excited I can feel it in my big toes. I get a little buzz and I know the blood is moving. I just felt it in my capillaries. Capillaries—ha, thank you for correcting me. Sometimes it's worth talking to you. You are annoying, but I've got to admit, you're smart as a ship.

CR: You mean smart as a whip.

TTTYOM: What the hell's so smart about a whip?

CR: Well, that's the expression.

TTTYOM: A ship I can see is smart. Turned out, on the water, anchors away, sails snapping, catching the wind . . . A ship looks smart. Smart as a ship makes sense.

CR: But the expression is—

TTTYOM: What? Smart as a whip? A whip just lays there, curled up in the corner. I would never say smart as a whip.

CR: Well, I understand you're paying me a compliment.

TTTYOM: Why not? You're smart as a ship.

CR: Thank you.

TTTYOM: You're welcome. And if people call you smart as a whip, correct them.

CR: I'll try. Sir, now that your blood is moving, let me ask you about another legend. Robin Hood. Did he really exist?

TTTYOM: Oh, yes. Lovely man. Ran around in the forest . . . in green tights. Very tight tights. You can see his *gantze geschicter*.*

CR: Did he really steal from the rich and give to the poor?

TTTYOM: No, he stole from everybody and kept everything.

CR: Then how did the legend start?

TTTYOM: He had a fella, Marty the press agent, who wrote in all the scrolls: "He took from the rich and gave to the poor." Who knew? He gave you such a knock on the head when he robbed you that you wouldn't remember anything anyway.

---

*Ed. *note:* The whole story.

CR: I hate to have legendary figures smashed like that.

TTTYOM: Well, I hate to smash them for you.

CR: What about King Arthur?

TTTYOM: A very important man. And not only a king. He owned four apartment buildings in downtown Camelot. He was some good businessman.

CR: And how about the Knights of the Round Table?

TTTYOM: No round table.

CR: There was no round table?

TTTYOM: Only when he ate with his family was there a round table. But when the knights came for dinner, they'd open it up and put in the leaves. Then it was King Arthur and the oval table.

CR: Is it true that in those days the knights were so gallant they'd really fight for a lady's handkerchief?

TTTYOM: Oh yes, a handkerchief was one of the big fights. When a lady would lose a handkerchief, two knights on horsies would run at each other with their long spears. They'd try to kill each other to get that handkerchief.

CR: But why?

TTTYOM: There was no Kleenex! They were wiping their noses on their sleeves. You heard the song "Greensleeves"? That's how it got its name. You know Rembrandt wrote that song?

CR: I thought it was written by Henry the Eighth?

TTTYOM: You're right. I always mistake them for each other. Rembrandt, Henry the Eighth, Charles Laughton—they all look alike to me. I think Charles Laughton played both of them in their movies.

CR: You knew Rembrandt?

TTTYOM: I sold him canvas and paints. Boy, did he use a lot of burnt umber. Did you know he was the first to use a roller?

CR: He painted with a roller?

TTTYOM: I sold it to him. Not the twelve-incher. The small one. But don't get the wrong idea. He only used it for the backgrounds. For introducing him to the roller, he gave me a small painting, a beauty: the *Night Watchman*.

CR: He gave you the *Night Watch*?

TTTYOM: No, the *Night Watch* is a masterpiece. You don't give away masterpieces so quick. He gave me a small drawing of the night watchman who guarded the *Night Watch*.

CR: Where is it now?

TTTYOM: I think it's in Boston. I gave it to my 365th wife, Abigail. She hung it in our kitchen over the icebox.

CR: You lived in Boston?

TTTYOM: From 1775 to 1777.

CR: During the Revolution?

TTTYOM: I lived on the same block as Paul Revere.

CR: Did you know him?

TTTYOM: An anti-Semite bastard.

CR: Paul Revere?

TTTYOM: He hated the Jews.

CR: That's never been reported.

TTTYOM: He was afraid the Jews were moving in. He worried that more were coming into the neighborhood.

"They're coming!" he yelled. Everybody heard him. "The Yiddish are coming! The Yiddish are coming!"

CR: No, no, no!

TTTYOM: Yes, yes, yes! All night he yelled, "The Yiddish are coming! The Yiddish are coming!"

CR: No, no, he was yelling, "The British are coming! The British are coming!"

TTTYOM: Not "the Yiddish"?

CR: No, "The British are coming."

TTTYOM: The British . . . ? Oy, my God! I didn't go to his funeral and I didn't send his wife a note. I'm going to have to apologize to all his great-great-great-great grandchildren.

PART II

Health & Food

CHAPTER XIX

Not Such a Top Doctor

 N THE EARLY days, people suffered with the same physical pains as they do today. Some groaned. Some went, "Whoooo!" Some went, "Haaaaaa!" Others went, "Ha-chi-chi! Ha-chi-chi!" Some screamed, "I don't need it, don't want it, but oy, here it comes again! Ahhhh!"

Everyone had different ways of dealing with pain. When it got overwhelming you went to see the one doctor who knew what to do, Dr. Poultice. That man was a genius! His idea was to make a bigger pain than was already there.

If you had a severe pain in your back, Dr. Poultice made up a mustard plaster with chili powder, black pepper, red pepper, green pepper, and lots of Tabasco. Then he smeared it all over your chest and immediately you screamed, "Ahhhhh! My chest! Ahhhhh!" You didn't feel the pain in your back anymore—just the pain in your chest.

What about that pain, you ask? Don't ever underestimate Dr. Poultice. He was brilliant. He took a big, heavy rock and smashed your foot. So then you hopped around, screaming, "Ohhh, my foot! Ohhh, my foot! Ohhh, my foot!"

And for that pain? Brilliant again. He stuck a twig in your eye which took your mind off your foot.

From then, you were screaming, "Ohhhhh, my eye! Ohhhhh, my eye!" Your foot, your chest, and your back you forgot about.

He was some doctor.

I recommended him to all my friends. I must admit, though, I never personally went to him myself. Once I heard about the twig in the eye treatment, I decided not to go to such a . . . *top* doctor. I didn't need such a specialist. I went to a neighborhood guy.

CHAPTER XX

The Blue Tongue Disease

HERE ARE NO diseases today's doctors know about that I haven't gotten, and I've had one or two that aren't on the big list they give you to check off.

When I lived in Vienna around the turn of the last century, I woke up one morning and, to amuse myself, as is my wont, I looked in the mirror, stuck out my tongue, and made a raspberry:

"BRRRRRRRR!"

I was shocked.

My tongue was all blue. I had a powder blue tongue. Sort of like a powder blue. Maybe it was cobalt. No, cobalt is too dark.

I know, robin's egg blue! That's the color. My tongue was

robin's egg blue, and I had no idea why. I know what you're thinking: Maybe I ate blueberries. I didn't. I know better. I scared myself once with beets. I'd forgotten I'd eaten them for lunch and that night when I looked in the bowl, everything was red, and I nearly panicked. From that day on, I don't eat anything with color.

When my tongue turned blue, I was lucky to be in a city like Vienna where there were many specialists, and even luckier to find the doctor who was just crossing over from the medical profession to the mental profession. Yes, I'm talking about the renowned Sigmund Freud. He was a strange cookie.

I told him my problem and I couldn't believe what he told me to do.

"You go over there and lie down on the couch," he said.

That made me nervous, and I said, "And what are *you* going to do?"

"I'm gonna sit in this chair behind you," he said.

"If you sit there and I lay here," I said, "how are you going to see my tongue?"

"I don't have to see your tongue," he replied. "I have to see what's inside your head."

"Well, Dr. Freud," I chuckled, "according to *my* copy of *Gray's Anatomy*, my tongue *is* in my head."

"Don't be smart," he snapped.

OK, so I lay down on the couch. For a while, he didn't say a word. Nothing. And I didn't say a word. Nobody talked. In those situations, I have an urge to laugh. But I suppressed it. I was too worried about my blue tongue. Finally he spoke.

"Tell me, what have you been eating lately?"

"I ate . . . what I always ate," I said. "I had matzo ball soup, a tongue sandwich, and a well-chilled celery tonic."

"That's it!" Freud exclaimed.

"The celery tonic?" I asked.

"No, the tongue sandwich!"

"That sounds a little nuts," I said. "No offense, Dr. Freud."

"Your tongue is depressed," he explained. "It's feeling blue, so it turned blue."

"Is that possible, Doctor?"

"Well, let's get into the mind of the tongue," he said.

"All right," I said skeptically. "Be my guest."

I thought the guy was a little *meshugah* but I was paying seven dollars an hour, so I went along.

"What is the tongue thinking?" Freud asked.

"OK, Doctor," I replied, "what is the tongue thinking?"

He said, "The tongue is thinking, This guy loves to eat tongue. I'm lying here in the middle of his mouth, teeth on all sides of me. I'm *vulnerable*!"

Believe it or not, it clicked. I agreed with him. From that day on, I didn't eat tongue. I switched to chopped liver. Immediately my tongue went from robin's egg blue to a normal pink, with a slight white covering which everyone has. Of course, I imagine my liver was nervous seeing all that chopped liver go by.

But I'm not worried about my liver turning blue. I say, If something turns blue and you don't see it, the hell with it.

CHAPTER XXI

Penicillin

 HE SPECIALISTS at UCLA and Cedars Sinai say it's amazing I've lived so long, considering all the diseases and plagues that have beset man in my time.

They were especially interested in the bubonic or black plague that I lived through in the fourteenth century, and they asked me to describe that terrible, terrible time. I didn't want to remember all the ugly details with the blotches and the diarrhea. So instead I gave them a short summation.

"Too many rats, not enough cats!"

At the time of the plague, I lived in southern France, which was then called the Bottom Part of Gaul. People were dying all around. Young, old, rich, poor. If it wasn't for Gedulia, my 167th wife, I wouldn't be here now. To this day, I have a love-hate memory of that woman.

Every house in the village had people dying from that lousy plague, but not ours because my wife was such a stingy miser. That woman never threw anything out. Every night she served leftover leftovers. Her specialty was moldy bread. I ate it because there was nothing else to eat. Was I lucky.

The green moldy bread turned out to be penicillin. My Gedulia beat Professor Alexander Fleming's discovery of penicillin by 600 years. A lot of people told me that I should take him to court. But if you'd ever met him, you'd know this was not a man you'd want to drag into a courtroom. This was a man to sit and have a cup of tea with and trade scientific information in a warm, friendly manner.

CHAPTER XXII

Homeopathy

 ECENTLY A newspaper reporter asked how I felt about homeopathy.

"I'm not against it," I said. "I'm a liberal guy. Let them do what they want. Far as I'm concerned, let them be in the Army. Let them be in Congress. Let them wear hoop skirts for all I care."

I probably wasn't listening carefully. I didn't really hear the word "homeopathy" that clearly. I just heard the "homeo" part. He was talking about alternative medicine—natural medicine with herbs and things like that. In my day, that's all we used. For instance, to cure crazy people, we used willow trees.

We peeled off its bark and boiled it in a pot of water over a fire. Then we took the juice and gave it to the lunatic.

If that didn't stop his violent behavior, we took a big branch from the tree and smashed him. That usually did the trick.

It was the whole basis of alternative medicine.

First try to help. Do your best.

If that doesn't work, hit them as hard as you can.

CHAPTER XXIII

Garlic

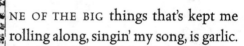

NE OF THE BIG things that's kept me rolling along, singin' my song, is garlic. It works on a simple principle.

The scientific reason you die is you get a visit from the Angel of Death. He usually comes late at night when you're sound asleep or just nodding off after your Ovaltine. He comes over to you, and says, "OK, Murray, this is it. Pucker up."

He's ready to give you the kiss of death.

So every night before I retire, I eat a good pound and a half of raw garlic. Then I lie down, pull up my crazy quilt, and start to snore.

When the Angel of Death taps me on the shoulder, I gather up a big breath and ask, "WHOOOO is it?"

He always goes, "PHEW!" holds his nose, and runs away fast. Last time he tried to get me I heard him mutter, "I don't care if I lose my job . . . I wouldn't kiss this guy for a million dollars."

CHAPTER XXIV

Prunes & More Secrets:
A Conversation

UST WHEN I thought Carl Reiner had asked me his last question, like Columbo he comes back and says, "Oh, just one more question, sir."

THE 2,000 YEAR OLD MAN: All right, what do you want to know, Mr. Pest?

CARL REINER: Sir, about your professed secrets to a long life. Many people have followed them and still they've passed away. Surely there must be other secrets that you know that will help us live a long and fruitful life.

TTTYOM: Fruit is good. Fruit kept me going for 140 years. Mainly nectarines. I love that fruit. It's half a peach, half a plum. It's a helluva fruit.

CR: I know.

TTTYOM: Not too cold, not too hot. Just nice. Even a rotten one is good. I'd rather eat a rotten nectarine than a fine plum. What do you think of that?

CR: I think you love nectarines a lot.

TTTYOM: More than you'll ever know. But I'll tell you there's a new fruit that's sneaking up on it—they call it a kiwi. Have you heard of it?

CR: Of course. It's from New Zealand.

TTTYOM: Boy, you're smart as a ship. The first time I saw a kiwi, I stabbed it. I tried to kill it. It looked like a sleeping mouse. I couldn't believe it turned out to be a fruit. And what a fruit! And when I tasted it, my tongue threw a party for my mouth.

CR: You liked it?

TTTYOM: All I can say is, "Nectarine, watch out."

CR: Is it just the fruit that makes for your longevity? Or do you avail yourself of the modern miracle drugs?

TTTYOM: I don't take drugs. I don't like them. I don't use them. I don't need them. And I don't buy them.

CR: So what do you use instead to ward off illness or disease?

TTTYOM: Like I said, fruits. The elixir of life.

CR: Are you saying that fruits can cure diseases?

TTTYOM: Absolutle. There's a fruit for every disease mankind has had. Name the disease, I'll give you the fruit.

CR: Arteriosclerosis?

TTTYOM: Bananas.

CR: Bananas?

TTTYOM: Bananas. Because arteriosclerosis is hardening of the arteries, you need something soft. Either bananas or a mushy pear. Either one will save you.

CR: How about tuberculosis?

TTTYOM: Blueberries. They stain the tubercular bacteria. You find them, and then you can kill them.

CR: How about . . . diarrhea?

TTTYOM: Peaches are very good for diarrhea.

CR: Any kind of peaches?

TTTYOM: No, not Elberta. You need the *cling* peaches.

CR: Do you have any other secrets?

TTTYOM: Prunes.

CR: Prunes? That's no secret. People have been eating prunes for—

TTTYOM: Did I say eat them? No. Soften the prunes in warm water till they look like a plum again. Place them on your eyeballs and let the prune water drip into your eyes and your ears.

CR: What does that do?

TTTYOM: I don't know. But it works for me. I'm still here. I say if prune juice can make you go, it can also make you stay. It's scientific and logical.

CR: "Prune" is a funny word, and I'm interested in the origin of words. Do you know why it's called a prune or why a plum is called a plum?

TTTYOM: A plum is plump. Take off the last "P" and you have a plum. Don't take off the first "P" or you'll have a lump.

CR: Why is a prune called a prune?

TTTYOM: What are you going to call it, a Buick? It's all wrinkled up and looks exactly like a prune. What else are you going to call it?

CR: What about the origin of the word "tomato"?

TTTYOM: Well, now you're asking me something that came out of a very embarrassing situation. I don't tell everybody, but I'm the guy who first called it a tomato.

CR: How did that come about?

TTTYOM: I was in Naples walking in the street with my wife Aida and I saw a beautiful girl walking toward us and without thinking, out of my mouth came, "Wow, what a beautiful tomato!" My wife said, "Are you talking about that beautiful girl?" "No, no," I said quickly. "Not the girl. I'm talking about the beautiful red thing she's eating." From that minute on, anytime I saw that red thing I called it a tomato. My wife bought into it. She started calling it a tomato, and soon all the *yentas* in the neighborhood called it a tomato. Was I lucky. You know, when I saw that girl I almost said, "What a beautiful ass." And she wasn't riding on anything . . .

CR: Do you know how cheese got its name?

TTTYOM: Sure, I know everything. Haven't you gleaned that by now? The word "cheese" originated 800 years ago. It came from a farmer. He stored some milk in a barrel outside. It was hot summer day, and he forgot about it. A week later, when he opened the barrel and stuck his head in, he said, "Cheezedoesthisstink!" For a while, everybody called it "cheezedoesthisstink!" People used to go into the

Cheezedoesthisstink Store and order a half a pound of cheezedoesthisstink. As time went on, it was shortened to what we know today, cheeze,* and now you find it in everything, all the fast foods—cheezeburgers,† pizza, and tacos . . .

CR: How do you feel about fast food?

TTTYOM: I don't like fast food.

CR: Why?

TTTYOM: I eat too slow.

CR: Since you've traveled the world and have eaten in every country, what is your favorite food?

TTTYOM: Jewish food, naturally.

CR: Which particular dishes?

TTTYOM: Chicken chow mein, moo goo gai pan, egg foo yung, fried rice . . . the traditional dishes.

CR: I guess it's true that the American Jews did make Chinese food popular. Why do you think that is? The delicacy of the cooking, the exotic vegetables, the flavorings?

TTTYOM: No, the prices. Years ago you could get one of these entire Jewish meals for 35 cents. And such a beautiful meal. You get your egg drop soup, your chicken chow mein, your white rice, your fortune cookie with

---

*Ed. *note:* Cheese.

---

†Ed. *note:* Cheeseburgers.

Author's *note:* This ed. is getting to be a pain in the ass.

your tea, and at the end of the meal they give you a ball of hard yellow ice cream with infinitesimal pieces of ice still in it.

CR: I remember that. Back in New York.

TTTYOM: You'd lick that spoon forever. But now unfortunately I don't eat that food anymore.

CR: Too high in cholesterol?

TTTYOM: No, too high in price. What used to be a nice Jewish meal became expensive Chinese food.

CR: By the way, do you drink?

TTTYOM: If I must.

CR: I mean alcohol. Wine.

TTTYOM: Yes, I'll take a sip or two now and then.

CR: Red or white?

TTTYOM: Pink. I'm partial to the chilled blush wines.

CR: Most people your age don't drink.

TTTYOM: What do you mean by "most" people? There's only me. Most people my age are dead.

CR: I read in *Time* magazine that the earliest wine dates back to 5,000 years B.C., and it was discovered by the Sumerians. Do you know about this?

TTTYOM: You call it wine, I call it *pishachs!** It was salty and undrinkable. The real wine came in 1524. In Italy. Made by Galileo.

CR: The astronomer?

---

*Ed. note: Piss.

TTTYOM: No. Two brothers. Ernest and Julio. They made the wine and did the packing and shipping, too. Those Galileo brothers were peppy guys.

CR: I think you'll find that it's the Gallo brothers.

TTTYOM: *Originally* it was the Galileo brothers. They changed their name because of the trouble. They didn't want to be associated with their other brother, the astronomer, because the Pope had it in for him.

CR: Because—

TTTYOM: Because he opened a mouth. I told him that he was crazy. But he said, "I have to say the truth. The sun doesn't move. The Earth moves around the sun." He asked me what I thought, and I said, "You're asking for it."

CR: It's a shame that Galileo was punished for a theory that was true.

TTTYOM: I'm not sure it's true. Think about it. If the Earth traveled around the sun and was spinning at such a high speed like he said, wouldn't we all be a little nauseous? And wouldn't a few children and small dogs fly off?

CR: What do you think of this astounding new space phenomenon?

TTTYOM: You mean the walk-in closet? So much space you can hang anything anywhere.

CR: No, I'm talking about the pictures they're sending back from Mars. What do you think of them?

TTTYOM: To me it looks a lot like Las Vegas before Bugsy Siegel got his hands on it.

CR: Well, you've managed to keep your feet on the ground. By the way, how do you feel about exercise?

TTTYOM: It's very tiring.

CR: But it has been proven to be beneficial.

TTTYOM: Sure, beneficial! Beneficial to the people who are making the NordicTrack, the StairMaster, the Buns of Steel, and the Tits of Titanium!

CR: As long as we're talking about health, there's been a lot written lately about early child development. *Time* and *Newsweek* have both written about how if you give love to a child in the early years of his life, he'll grow up to be a functioning, nourishing human being.

TTTYOM: True, true, true, true.

CR: You believe it?

TTTYOM: How many trues did I give you?

CR: Four.

TTTYOM: Well, would I give four trues if I didn't believe it? Love is critical. Right at the beginning a child should have plenty of it. Even before the beginning.

CR: How could it be before the beginning?

TTTYOM: When your child is still in your wife's belly, talk to it. Say, "I love you, whoever you are in there. I love you." That child hears that. That child hears everything. You think the child doesn't hear when the father comes home drunk late at night and the wife says, "You drunken skunk, spent your whole paycheck with those bums at the bar?" The unborn baby worries.

CR: I'd like to ask about some of the great people in history you've known—whether as children they were given the love and attention that would make them great people. For instance, I assume Shakespeare must've been hugged.

TTTYOM: Absolutle. Hugged, kissed, and bit on the tushy. There was a lot of love there. How else could a fella make up such wonderful phrases like, "But soft, what yonder light broke my window."

CR: How about Mahatma Gandhi?

TTTYOM: Loved to pieces. They loved that baldy baby. They never even bought him a pair of pants. They kept him in diapers all his life. That's how much they adored him.

CR: What about Richard Nixon?

TTTYOM: Hugged. But mainly by Sammy Davis, Jr.

CR: Well, obviously Ivan the Terrible was not hugged.

TTTYOM: No, not hugged. If Ivan had been hugged, he'd probably have been known as Ivan the Not-So-Terrible. And if he'd been kissed, he might have even turned out to be Ivan the Likable.

CR: What about Lizzie Borden?

TTTYOM: You don't make your parents into a Waldorf salad if you've been hugged and kissed.

CR: Susan B. Anthony?

TTTYOM: Susan was not only hugged and kissed, she was also licked.

CR: Licked?

TTTYOM: Sure—when she became a stamp.

CR: How about Marilyn Monroe?

TTTYOM: Hugged a lot after she was Marilyn Monroe, but not hugged enough as Norma Jean . . . sadly.

CR: Moses?

TTTYOM: Hugged.

CR: Buddha?

TTTYOM: Hugged.

CR: Hitler?

TTTYOM: Mugged. Not hugged. No one read to him. No one bought him an ice cream cone in the summer. No one ever said, "Dolfie, would you like Papa to read *Goodnight Moon* again?" I've always said if someone—a mother, a father, a good-looking neighbor, anyone—had said, "Oy, is this a darling little boy-and-a-half or what?" maybe instead of sending buzz bombs to London he would've sent flowers to his little girlfriend next door. There was probably no love in the Hitler family for centuries. Look how no hugging and no kissing can make a whole world suffer. So keep hugging and kissing your kids—even if they say, "Stop already."

CHAPTER XXV

Homilies—True or False

I N MY LONG and wonderful life, I have discovered that most of the clichés, sayings, and homilies are not true. All these catchy statements that are meant to pass for wisdom are actually the work of a sixteenth-century greengrocer from England. His name was Clement Bartlett, and he had a little store called Bartlett's Quotations and Pears, where he sold books and pears.

1. TRUE or FALSE:
The apple doesn't fall far from the tree.

FALSE. Apples can fall very far from a tree. If it's on a hill, the apple could roll for miles.

2. TRUE or FALSE:
There's more than one way to skin a cat.

FALSE. There's only one way to skin a cat—you grab it by the nose and you pull backward with all your might. Never do it at night, otherwise you'll wake up the whole village. Early afternoon is preferable.

3. TRUE or FALSE:
A *stitch in time saves nine.*

FALSE. It saves one. However, nine stitches in time will save nine.

4. TRUE or FALSE:
A *penny saved is a penny earned.*

RIDICULOUS. A penny saved is a penny saved. A penny earned is a penny earned. But who cares? You're talking pennies here. However, a million saved is two million earned if you bought Microsoft at eleven.

5. TRUE or FALSE:
A *rolling stone gathers no moss.*

FALSE. If it rolls very, very, very slowly, it will gather moss. Not a lot, but enough to spoil Mr. Bartlett's cliché.

6. TRUE or FALSE:
The early bird catches the worm.

TRUE. But who cares? I'd rather have that delicious sleep you get from six to eight-thirty in the morning. Besides—I love cornflakes, and I hate worms.

7. TRUE or FALSE:
It's better to give than to receive.

WRONG. I'd rather receive an egg salad sandwich than to give away a hundred dollars.

8. TRUE or FALSE:
What goes around comes around.

It could be TRUE or it could be FALSE, and to tell you the truth I don't know what the hell it means. You have to live longer than me to figure that one out. Even Alex Trebek* doesn't have the answer to that one, and he's got those little cards.

---

*Ed. *note:* Host of *Jeopardy,* a syndicated TV game show.

Author's note: Merv Griffin sold it to Sony but they still let him be the producer. I think he still gets a few bucks from it. Who knows?

PART III

Modern Life:
Today & Tomorrow

CHAPTER XXVI

If You Know the Extension, Press One . . .
(Pet Peeves)

I DON'T KNOW ABOUT you, but I hate when I'm stuck in traffic and the guy next to me rolls down the window and plays that boom-bang-bing box stereo so loud with a rap song that has a guy singing, "Do it with your bitch till somebody dies . . ."

I don't have to hear that song.

It's not even a song. It's somebody just declaring:

> Jimmy, Jimmy, Jimmy/
> gimme, gimme, gimme/
> do me, do me, do me/
> screw me, screw me, screw me . . .

Very little creativity there. To me, it's the opposite of Cole Porter. (No "trip to the moon on gossamer wings" there.)

But there's something I hate even more than the rap music. It's when you make a phone call and hear, "If you know your party's extension, press one. If you don't know your party's extension, press two. If you know anybody's extension, press three."

You can't get a human being.

"Press six if you want your pants pressed."

"If this is an emergency, press 911."

"If you are bleeding from the eye, press two. If you're bleeding from your tushy, press four . . ."

You can press all day and you'll never get a human person.

I say you'll do better going back to the old-fashioned ways. If something terrible happens and you need assistance, pick up your telephone and throw it through your window, stick your head out of the hole and scream: "Somebody! I need help! And don't call 911! Just come up here!"

CHAPTER XXVII

Smells & Sex

IRST LET'S TALK SMELLS.
Today people worry about their
rights and freedoms. Some want more.
Some want less. I'm more concerned that
they're taking away our individual smells.
It's terrible.

There's a spritz or a spray for everything. Under the arms.
In the nose. In the crotch. You have no idea who you're talking to anymore. You don't know the difference between men
and women. Everybody smells like a strawberry. You walk
past a fruit stand and you get hot. What the hell is that?

That's no way to live.

Now a word about sex.

Since my last wife passed away and then died, about

ninety years ago, I have had some difficulty connecting with a person of the opposite sex. I was frustrated until a neighbor taught me how to use his computer, and a new window opened on my life.

We're not talking Internet, we're talking computer sex. I fell head over heels in love with Dot Com—short for Dorothy Comsky, my computer girlfriend. And then, as exciting as it was, it fell apart, as love will.

Being honest is not always the best policy. She confessed her age and so I confessed mine. I should've never told her I was 2,037. The last e-mail I got from her said, "It's over. It won't work. I'm only eighty-nine. It's too much of an age difference."

CHAPTER XXVIII

Shopping Malls

 VERYONE HANGS OUT at the shopping malls. I don't go. I hate them.

They're a blight. It's impossible to find a store there. I mean, a real, honest-to-goodness store. Where you can get an egg cream* or a long pretzel.

There's no stores. Only boutiques. And a million shoe stores. You got the Shoe Box, the Foot Locker, Feet First, and a new one—the Athlete's Foot.

---

*Author's note: No egg, no cream, just chocolate syrup, seltzer, and sometimes a splash of milk.

Look at that—they named a store after a fungus.

They've got shoes for everything—jogging, running, walking . . . And God forbid you should ever get caught walking in your running shoes. The shoe police will give your feet a ticket.

CHAPTER XXIX

The Environment

 IKE OTHER PEOPLE, I worry constantly about the so-called greenhouse effect. Every year the world's temperature increases in small increments. In my own lifetime, I've seen it go from mild to warm to hot. A lot of people are trying to do something about it. Saving our environment is one of the wonderful causes I believe in. Last year I gave twelve dollars anonymously to my favorite charity, Out Goes the Bad Air, In Comes the Good Air, Inc. That's how concerned I am.

My great fear is that the temperature will continue to rise. If it does, it will be a disaster. I'll have absolutely no use for my entire winter wardrobe.

CHAPTER XXX

Crime of the Century

 VERYBODY ASKS ME, "What did you think of the Crime of the Century?"

The hackles are still going up at the back of my neck. That those idiots gave Audrey Hepburn Julie Andrews's role in the movie *My Fair Lady* after she sang it on Broadway for two years—to me, that's the crime of the century!

Where's the justice?

Audrey Hepburn didn't even sing.

They had to get someone from the President's family to sing for her. Marni Nixon. Must be a niece or something. There, now everybody knows the truth.

I'm upset to this day.

Unfortunately most people don't share my outrage. They're upset with what they think is the Crime of the Century—the O. J. Simpson Trial. They're wrong. That trial enriched the nation.

Yes, an event like that, in its own strange way, helped the whole country. Look at all the money publishers paid for books by the trial's participants: Johnnie Cochran got $2 million. Christopher Darden got $1 million. Marcia Clark got $4 million. Mark Fuhrman got $2 million. Robert Shapiro got $1 million. Paula Barbieri got $4 million. That's a grand total of $14 million.

I haven't even taken into account the money that publishers paid to Faye Resnick, Alan Dershowitz, and O. J. himself! Altogether it's probably forty or fifty million dollars, the government takes half of that, which means $25 million. And boy, can Uncle Sam use it. With $25 million, he can fill a few potholes, put a couple of computers in schools that can't afford them, and maybe spend a little more money on the White House barbershop so the president of the United States doesn't have to go flying off to Beverly Hills for a good haircut.

CHAPTER XXXI

A Few of
My Favorite Things

VERY TIME I mention Julie Andrews, I can't help but think of a few of my favorite things. Here they are:

My favorite movie? It's a toss-up between Jean Renoir's *Grand Illusion* and *Debbie Does Dallas*. I admire them both but for different reasons. They're both very emotional and both reveal the naked truth about life, each in its own way.

My favorite play? *Antony and Cleopatra*. Not the one

Shakespeare wrote. The real version. I was traveling through Egypt and there was Cleopatra and Antony on a barge. The original cast. I watched them kissing for an hour until one of the guards came over and said, "OK, buddy, move along. Show's over."

CHAPTER XXXII

Great Discoveries

AS FAR AS GREAT modern discoveries go, I still have a warm spot in my heart for Saran Wrap. You can still wrap a sandwich in it, look through it, touch it, and put it over your face. You can still make a small one and put three olives in it or a big one with ten sandwiches.

Big or little—doesn't matter. It clings. It's still fantastic.

But something's been developed that's even more remarkable—Velcro!

It's based on both a scientific and a psychological principle. Narcissism.

It loves itself.

You can't get it apart. It's all over itself.

In my mind, it's responsible for all the great achievements in space. When they go to space, things rattle around, and so they put Velcro over everything and it keeps the telescopes and all the Phillips screwdrivers in their right place.

It's amazing.

I hate to sound like I'm knocking Saran Wrap, but believe me, it doesn't compare to Velcro. Take them both on vacation and see which one is more valuable. The minute something rattles around in the back of my van, I Velcro it. If two boxes of Saran Wrap are bouncing around, I Velcro them together.

However, exciting as the discovery of Velcro is, I'd be remiss if I didn't bring to your attention a new innovative invention that I think is one of the greatest breakthroughs of modern science—the swirl!

I loved it when nonfat and lo-cal frozen yogurt were discovered. But when they made that spout that can put two different flavors into one cone, it made my heart sing. I'm a plain Jane. I always tell them to swirl chocolate and vanilla for me. But you can get a peach and praline swirl. Or you can get a pineapple cheesecake and passion fruit swirl. Or even an Oreo cookie and cappuccino swirl. There's no end to the exotic combinations.

I just read in *Popular Mechanics* that they're working on a triple swirl. But I don't think I'll see it in my lifetime, and if I don't see it in my lifetime you can forget about seeing it in yours. Either way, watch out, Saran Wrap and Velcro, the swirl is right behind you.

CHAPTER XXXIII

Words of Wisdom

 F ALL THE ADVICE I can give, here's one that you'll always be grateful that I imparted to you: When you're riding in an airplane and you have to go to the toilet, be careful!

After you do your business, and before flushing, put down that cover because on the new model jet planes the flush is so powerful it could rip your wallet out of your pants and all your loose change—and your keys could go flying in there, too. You'll never see them again, unless you're staying at a Ramada Inn. For some reason that key always finds its way back.

CHAPTER XXXIV

Cloning
(Peace on Earth)

WHEN I HEARD a couple of scientists in Scotland had cloned a sheep, I became extremely upset by the threat it posed to civilization. Nothing in my life had ever gotten me so worried, and I could remember plenty of times when I feared for the future of mankind.

What they did to this sheep! It was frightening. The sheep was the first mammal ever created without a father. There was no sex involved! Without permission, two scientists took a dot of DNA from a lady sheep, placed it into another sheep's egg from which the nucleus had been removed, and shoved it in a surrogate ewe. She gave birth to a little lamb who everyone said looked exactly like her mother.

It was all done with tweezers, rubber gloves, and test tubes.

There was no touching, no cute looks, not even a bunch of flowers, and not a single, "Ooh-ooh, baby."

There wasn't one minute of foreplay.

Can you imagine if you did that with people? People work hard all week and they live for two things: getting off on Friday afternoon, and getting off on Saturday night. You take that away from them, you're going to have some very nervous people. Part of the sexual act is a drive to release all the emotions, frustrations, and hotness in us—hotness that has got to be cooled down.

It's the same with sheep.

If we don't let them do what comes naturally, I guarantee there's going to be big trouble ahead.

People have to be people and animals have to be animals.

It's a law of nature, and unlike Prohibition this is a law even Congress can't repeal.

In today's world, scientists are all working hard to create smaller microchips and bigger potato chips, and I say what they're emphasizing is all *fakakht.**

One thing I know—all of life's problems will not be solved by designer drugs or liposuction. No, sir. No matter how many new and improved liquid soaps or antacid pills they develop, life will always be filled with its booby traps, torments,

---

*Ed. *note:* All screwed up.

and nuisances. Seven hundred years ago, during a locust plague, I coined the phrase "Shit happens," and it stuck because it's true. Mothers always call at the wrong time. You can't eat a jelly donut without your hands getting sticky. And there will always be a jerk who doesn't move far enough into the intersection before making a left-hand turn. These are the annoying facts of life.

But in between, there is plenty to celebrate. We have poetry, music, dance, and now bagel shops on every corner. Like I once said to Gertrude Stein, "A rose is a rose, and you can't do better than a dozen of them to Alice on Valentine's Day."

My advice is to slow down, relax, and smell the lox and onions.

The reason we're all here is no mystery. Scientists can stop looking.

Life is about one thing, and one thing only.

Love.

That's what I'm talking about. Love.

L-O-V-E.

It's not just a many-splendored thing. It's *the* splendored thing.

For that reason I predict that if we don't keep our noses out of the sheep's private parts and prevent them from releasing their pent-up hotness by having sex, there will be bands of marauding sheep roaming the planet, terrorizing townships, attacking villages, and destroying big cities. They will wipe out civilization as we know it.

I say: Let the sheep hump! Let us have peace in our time!

BOOK BONUS

Contents of the Table

CHAPTER XXXV

The 2,000 Year Old Man's Seven-Day Diet

IKE MANY OF YOU, I have struggled with a weight problem all my life. I've eaten everything and everywhere, so who better than me, the 2,037 year old man, to come up with a surefire way to obtain your desired weight?

After much research, using myself as a guinea chicken,* I have developed a simple seven-day regimen that is both safe

---

*Ed. note: Guinea pig.

Author's note: Being kosher, pig is out of the question.

and nutritious and you won't feel deprived. If you follow it seriously, I guarantee success. Twenty-two people have already tried my diet and have realized big changes in their weight. Obese people lose a lot, and thin people gain a little.

It's an all-around diet, an exciting one for those people who will try any new diet that comes along.

All I ask is that you try as best you can to eat all your meals at the same time each day and in a pleasant environment. Enjoy your food, eat slowly, and chew well.

Shall we diet?

Day One Menu

Nothing.

On your table place an empty eight-ounce glass and an empty twelve-inch dinner plate. Utensils optional. Napkin with napkin ring optional.

Day Two

Three raisins
Eight ounces of water

All three raisins should be eaten at one time before noon, either for breakfast or brunch.

The eight ounces of water should be consumed in the following manner: four ounces with breakfast, three ounces for lunch, and one ounce for dinner.

IMPORTANT: *Eight ounces must be consumed before bedtime to ensure noninterrupted sleep because if you have to get up to pee you may be starving and tempted to break your diet.*

Day Three

Six raisins
Two eight-ounce glasses of water

Breakfast:

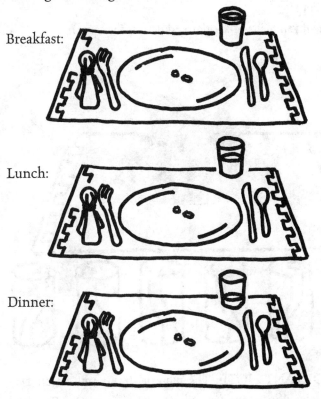

Lunch:

Dinner:

Raisins should be divided into three equal meals: two raisins per meal.

Eight ounces of water with breakfast, six ounces of water with lunch, and only two ounces of water with dinner . . . and you know why.

Day Four

A **HUGE sky-high** pastrami sandwich
(with cole slaw and Russian dressing)
Six Diet Pepsis
(*Diet Coke if you prefer—the calorie content is the same*)

IMPORTANT NOTE: *The more pastrami you eat on Day Four, the more efficient the diet will be. I predict that Day Four will be your favorite day.**

Ed. note: Photo of actual pastrami sandwich courtesy Carnegie Deli, 854 Seventh Avenue, New York, NY. Open Sundays.

Day Five

Nothing.
(*If you've followed the diet earnestly, Day Four's intake should carry you through Day Five.*)
Note: One to four Rolaids if necessary.

Day Six

One twelve-inch pineapple cheesecake
> *or*

one twelve-inch chocolate cheesecake.
> (*But not both. By eating both, you can destroy the good work you've done.**)

Strawberry Kiwi Snapple (*chilled*)
> Drink as much Snapple as you need to get the cheesecake down.

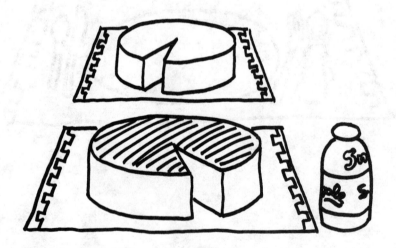

---

*Author's note: Listen, if you know in your heart that you're going to eat both cheesecakes, do me a favor and don't even start this diet. It's people like you—obsessive, compulsive, out-of-control mani-acs—that can make my wonderful diet look like another crazy diet that doesn't work.

Day Seven

A large organic health salad of arugula, romaine lettuce, endive, radicchio, shredded carrots, and broccoli florets. Toss with a fat-free dressing of balsamic vinegar, horseradish, salt-free Dijon mustard, dill weed, and cilantro.
Beverage: Eight ounces of orange-flavored Crystal Geyser water.

Dessert: A sky-high pastrami sandwich.

Optional: You may skip the salad if you prefer to eat your dessert first.

As you know, there are more diet books than dieters, among them the Atkins diet, the Stillman diet, the Scarsdale diet, the Zone diet, the grapefruit diet, the Drinking Man's diet, the Eating Man's diet, the Sleeping Man's diet, the Beverly Hills diet, the Akron, Ohio diet, the Mayo Clinic diet, the Hold the Mayo diet, and the latest, the Nothing But Prunes and Kaopectate diet.

Like me, you've probably tried them all. I guarantee that if you go on the 2,000 Year Old Man diet for seven days, you'll end up losing weight and keeping it off at least two days before shooting back up to your normal overweight weight— plus three more pounds that you don't know where the hell they came from. Look at it this way, as you probably always do, those three pounds are a blessing in disguise. They will motivate you to go on a diet.

If you have any questions of any kind whatsoever about this book, please don't annoy me with them; call the publishers—that's what they're for.